Instructor's Manual to Accompany

ELEMENTS OF

ARGUMENT

A Text and Reader
ANNETTE T. ROTTENBERG

Instructor's Manual to Accompany

ELEMENTS OF ARGUMENT

A TEXT AND READER

Annette T. Rottenberg

A Bedford Book

St. Martin's Press · New York

PREFACE

In this manual I have assembled some of the assignments and classroom
activities that have proved successful over the years in illuminating the
elements of argument and eliciting thoughtful student response. Every
teacher will have a collection of favorite devices, and I claim no superiority for mine. If some of the materials are not suitable, they may,
however, suggest other kinds that are. Together with the writing suggestions in the text and the anthology they should provide an ample repertory
of things to do for every day of the course. Clearly there will be more
material than any single class can profitably use. But I keep in mind
what a wise supervising teacher long ago gave me as one of her secrets for
confidence in the classroom: "Always be overprepared."
    The text is flexible. Students usually need or want more practice in
some areas than others. If the use of support, for example, is one element in which the majority of students are weak, you may want to spend
more time on the material in Chapter 4 and omit an extended discussion of
language and fallacies. The heart of the text is, of course, Chapters 2,
3, 4, and 5. Remaining Chapters 6 and 7 can be handled less intensively.
    Opposing Viewpoints lends itself to formal debate and longer papers
that incorporate research and analyze in-depth the opposing arguments--a
unit on debate is outlined in the manual. However, this chapter-by-
chapter section can also be used throughout the course as a reference
guide for papers that fulfill different kinds of writing assignments. The
anthology, too, is an additional source of arguments for study and reference.
    The linear organization of the course should pose no problems. It
is true that from the first assignment students will be writing argu-
ments--before they have completed the study of the elements of argument.
This practice, however, is the same as that of any other composition
course where the process is one of deepening, widening, and enriching a
first draft or a series of undeveloped generalizations. Many teachers of

Preface

composition, myself among them, believe that students should begin to write whole essays from the beginning of the course. Attention to the components of argument follows when students attempt to make their essays stronger by concentrating on the particular areas that need development and revision.

CONTENTS

Contents

PART ONE

THE STRUCTURE OF ARGUMENT

Chapter 1

INTRODUCTION TO ARGUMENT

1.   For years, ever since I began to teach argumentation, I have been a passionate clipper of articles from every available source on the subjects that we are likely to discuss in class or use as assignment topics. I invite students and colleagues to contribute to the collection, which now numbers about forty different subjects. The materials in these files also serve as a backup resource for students who are unable to find articles in the library on popular subjects such as abortion, euthanasia, gun control, etc., because the materials have been removed by overzealous researchers.

    I also use the clippings to introduce a unit, displaying articles that point to problems connected with definitions or hidden assumptions or fallacious reasonings. Students always show a good deal of interest in the clippings, which represent "real life" and report recent research findings of which they may be unaware.

2.   After discussion of the exercises at the end of the chapter, assign a brief search through newspapers and magazines (beginning perhaps with the school newspaper) for arguments about current affairs. Such a search enables students to arrive at several important conclusions.

    (a)   The most obvious one is that arguments of the kind they will be reading and writing in class are to be found everywhere and that they are the foundation of the democratic process. Students will also discover that a good deal of the factual reporting about political events is reporting of controversies or arguments.

    (b)   Without much familiarity with formal arguments, students may at first regard them all as vehicles of reasoned analysis. As they reflect on their examples, they will

3

        recognize that passion and ideology are formidable--sometimes the only--components of many arguments.

(c)   Many, perhaps most, freshman students believe that hardcore problems in our society remain unsolved because, at best, we lack the will to solve them, or, at worst, evil people conspire to frustrate attempts at solution. One other explanation of our failures may not readily occur to them: lack of knowledge. We may ask: What kind of knowledge--that is, data and interpretation of data--do we need in order to solve apparently intractable problems of poverty, war, prejudice, crime, mental illness? When we introduce this question, we may find that some students think that these problems are new and peculiar to American society. Much of the information needed will turn out to be psychological, the kind most difficult to discover or verify. (As I write this, a newspaper headline asserts, "Traits Shared by Mass Killers Remain Unknown to Experts.") I use this discussion to encourage a reflective caution when evaluating and advocating solutions.

(d)   Not all arguments have two equally valid sides. Some have multiple sides. Others may be said to have only one morally acceptable side. Ask students to suggest subjects that exemplify these conclusions.

3.   Students may be asked to keep informal journals that list argumentative subjects appearing in newspapers and magazines, on TV and radio, on the campus and in town. For each subject they may set down some of the important facts, values, and general principles underlying the claims. The journal entries can then serve as a source of subjects for assignments or discussion in class and in conferences with the instructor. A worthwhile dividend of such journal keeping is an increase in the practice of reading and listening, of becoming familiar with the sources and subjects of public controversies.

4.   I would leave discussion and analysis of the three major elements of argument--claim, support, and warrant--to the subsequent chapters. At this point I would require only that students show understanding of the definitions.

5.   In speech classes students sometimes analyze their audience, i.e., their classmates, before making a proposal that might be unpopular. They distribute questionnaires that they themselves have constructed in an effort to discover the social and political preferences of their classmates. The results of the questionnaire help them to choose an argumentative strategy that will persuade this audience to look more favorably on the proposition being argued.

     An application of this procedure for a writing class might work as follows: At the beginning of the semester, after having read about audience, a small group of students, perhaps four or five, make up an informal questionnaire which is filled out by the members of the class. The results of the questionnaire are

4

tabulated and distributed to the class. Later in the semester, for selected papers, e.g., arguments of policy, the writers are encouraged to examine the results and add a note describing how and why they have adapted their arguments to the values of this particular audience.

Chapter 2

CLAIMS

CLAIMS OF FACT

1.   Students have little difficulty understanding claims of fact. But before giving an assignment, I offer a dozen or more examples of such claims to make clear what kinds of arguments they produce. These are in addition to examples in the book.

2.   If students have already elected a major or are about to do so, they can find subjects in their areas of specialization. At this point library research need not be emphasized. Students are often able to find sufficient factual data in their memories or their notes. (Wherever possible, they should, of course, give credit to their sources, even to a lecturer in an academic course.)

        I point out that the reports they may be asked to make on the job are often claims of fact, in which the students provide proof that a condition exists or that something has been found to be true as a result of research. The thesis statements of their class essays correspond to the conclusions of their reports, which, like the theses, may appear first. Example (in an article about food colorants): "The development of organic chemistry produced a series of compounds that are well suited to coloring food. Today most of the food colorants are chemicals produced by synthesis from simple basic materials." (A Progress Report, Massachusetts Agricultural Station, July-August 1974.)

        Such straightforward factual reports are not likely to be models of creativity, but they emphasize other important qualities of good writing: adequate support, a direct, unadorned style, and clear transitions between ideas. They offer practice in the kind of clear exposition that all writers are well advised to master before they go further.

3.   More challenging are factual claims that are clearly controversial. Some will require only reflection on personal observation as support; others will need objective data. Examples: "The students on this campus are increasingly conservative." "Teaching writing on the word processor will not produce better writers." "Children are now judged to be reliable witnesses in child-abuse cases."

"Attractive people are regarded by others as more intelligent and sensitive than unattractive people."

Encourage students to stick to the facts and avoid direct expression of value judgments (although, of course, they may be implicit).

4.   Another source of assignments may be the materials in Opposing Viewpoints. Ask students to choose one of the subjects and, after reading all or most of the selections, derive a limited factual claim. Examples: "Animal experimentation has provided enormous medical benefits for human beings." "In analyzing pornography, women and men seem to have different concerns."

The supporting materials will not be original. This assignment tests the writer's ability to extract relevant data in support of a thesis, express the facts in his or her own language, and organize them logically.

Readings in the Anthology

(For comments on the use of these essays, please see the discussions for the anthology in this manual.)

"The Health-Care System"
"Where College Fails Us"
"Stereotype Truth"
"Politics and the English Language"
"Test-Tube Babies: Solution or Problem?"

The first part of this essay is purely factual and establishes that the procedure is risky.

CLAIMS OF VALUE

1.   As they begin to write, students will discover that the line between claims of fact and claims of value is often blurred, but in real-life arguments outside the classroom, these distinctions are not crucial. We make them in the classroom largely because they allow us to examine the elements more closely.

2.   Claims of value are more demanding than claims of fact. Facts remain important, but now students must express an attitude toward them. Despite the fact that values are a part of almost every argument--even in claims of fact they may be implicit in the choices of subjects and data--students are sometimes unclear about how to uncover and express them. These approaches may be helpful:

(a)   Ask personal questions. What do you want out of life? Do you dislike anything about yourself? Do you have religious beliefs? If so, how do they influence your behavior? What are the good things about your family? What are the most valuable things you own? What kind of country do you want

the United States to be? And so on. (Of course, for purposes of the exercise the answers need not be true, and it
should be clear to students that they are under no obliga-
tion to bare their souls. On the other hand, most students,
like the rest of us, enjoy talking about themselves.)

The answers that emerge can be written on the board,
listed as positive and negative values. You will probably
have to change the language, finding more precise terms
than the ones that the students offer. This exercise de-
fines values and value systems in a readily understandable
way. Values as a form of support will be discussed more
fully in Chapter 4, but this discussion should assist students to find the values that can be defended in their
value claims.

(b)   Analyze one or two essays in the text to discover the val-
       ues of the author. Take "It's Failure, Not Success" by
       Ellen Goodman. What traits in people does Goodman admire?
       What traits does she dislike? How do you know? How would
       you define her value system?

       I ask students to answer such questions in short, in-
       class assignments--fifteen minutes--for which they must
       produce a well-organized paragraph: clear topic sentence
       and sufficient supporting material. Since they stress
       economy and directness, such assignments are useful for
       teaching some elements of style.

3.   As with claims of fact, students can draw on campus experience for
     subjects that lend themselves to class discussion, outlining, and
     reinforcing the ways in which claims of value differ from claims
     of fact. Examples: "Student evaluations of teachers are worth-
     less." "Funds for Gay Awareness Week are unjustified."

4.   In this unit, too, I point out that claims of value are often re-
     quired on the job in the form of personnel reports or reports that
     evaluate marketing strategies and campaigns. If students are in-
     terested, topics for such papers can be obtained from books on
     technical writing or from the business departments of the school.

Readings in the Anthology

(For comments on the use of these essays, please see the discussions for
the anthology in this manual.)

"The Ignored Lesson of Anne Frank"
"It's Failure, Not Success"
"I Have a Dream"
"The Penalty of Death"
"The War of the Woods"
"Socrates to His Accusers"
"The Case for Torture"

(text pages 24-53)

"Test-Tube Babies: Solution or Problem?"
    The second part of this essay argues against the values that promote
parenthood at any cost.
"The Indispensable Opposition"

CLAIMS OF POLICY

1.   Since claims of policy assert that something should or should not
        be done, they presuppose the existence of a problem needing solu-
        tion. I emphasize that both facts and values are indispensable to
        defense of a policy claim because in many arguments students will
        first have to establish that a problem exists, then underscore how
        the desired values will be served by adoption of the proposed solu-
        tion.
2.   As an introduction to this unit, short problems, either real or
        hypothetical, can test the ability of students to find solutions--
        that is, to defend claims of policy. The facts are clearly laid
        out in the summary of the problem. In order to justify the solu-
        tion, students will need to expose the values that underlie their
        claims. Example of a real problem:

                        "The Plagiarism Problem"

            John Jones, a senior at U--- M----, was enrolled in a second-
        semester writing course, Writing About Film. A few weeks be-
        fore the end of the semester he suffered a crisis in his love
        life. The woman who had been his inseparable companion sud-
        denly informed him that she was no longer interested in con-
        tinuing their friendship. John lost control of himself for a
        few weeks; he stayed in his room brooding, drank heavily
        every night, and stopped going to classes. Three days before
        the end of the semester, he found out that in order to pass
        the film course and then to graduate, he had to fulfill a
        final assignment--attend a film and write a review of it.
        Frantic, John went to the library, copied out a review of a
        film by a professional critic, and submitted it to the in-
        structor. The instructor recognized the plagiarism and failed
        John for the course. The failure meant that John could not
        graduate despite the fact that he had a job waiting for him
        in Seattle. He argued with the instructor to no avail. The
        instructor said that he had made it very clear from the begin-
        ning of the semester that any plagiarism would result in a
        failure for the course. John appealed to the Provost, who had
        the authority to grant a Pass for the course.

8

Question: Should the Provost rule that John need not do anything more to fulfill the writing course and allow him to graduate?

3.   I have called attention to this problem in the text, but perhaps it
bears repeating. In defending claims of policy, students must
guard against offering solutions for enormous problems that have
defied solutions for decades or even centuries. Their ambitions
may be laudable, but nevertheless, they should be urged to confine
themselves to solutions that can be defended in 750 words.

4.   Opposing Viewpoints is a collection of problems in search of solutions. Assign readings in any of the subjects and ask students to
propose solutions based on their evaluations of the arguments.
        In defending their claims of policy students should try to
use the pattern of organization we call defending the stock is-
sues--need, plan, and advantage (see Appendix, Writing an Argumentative Essay). This pattern permits them to be exhaustive without
becoming confused by a multitude of details and a variety of possible approaches.

5.   Policy claims are, of course, inherent in any business or professional activity. Ask students who have job experience to write out
short summaries of specific problems they remember having encoun-
tered on the job, either their own or someone else's. The problems
should be substantive, and the facts should be clearly stated.
Then ask other students to suggest solutions. Students may also
ask for examples of problems from the business departments of the
school.
        These short writing exercises emphasize clarity, accuracy, and
a sensitivity to the audience--the employer, supervisor, or other
employees--who will act on the decision.
        If the solutions differ, students may discuss the differences
and try to uncover the reasons for them. Do the differences derive from lack of sufficient data or from conflicting values? Can
the differences be reconciled?

Readings in the Anthology

(For comments on the use of these essays, please see the discussions for
the anthology in this manual.)

"A Proposal to Abolish Grading"
"Homosexuality: Tolerance Versus Approval"
"The Case for Torture"
"The Indispensable Opposition"
"A Modest Proposal"
"Drugs"

(text pages 54-74)

"Test-Tube Babies: Solution or Problem?"
    The central claim is that test-tube babies should not be considered
the only acceptable alternative for infertile couples.

Chapter 3

DEFINITION

1.   I often begin this unit by dividing the class into four or five
        groups and assigning to each group the definition of a common ob-
        ject--book, bed, chair, cup, shoe. The definitions that emerge
        from the group are then compared to those in the dictionary. (The
        definitions by students are often remarkably close.)
            After this exercise I ask students to describe the process of
        definition they have just engaged in. As the discussion proceeds,
        students discover, first of all, that in matters of definition we
        know more than we can tell. (See Michael Polanyi's fascinating
        examination of this in The Tacit Dimension.) Apart from this phil-
        osophical dilemma, the attempt to define these familiar objects
        gives practice in distinguishing the properties that separate sim-
        ilar objects or objects belonging to the same genres. Equally im-
        portant, students must think of examples if they are to make useful
        distinctions--between a shoe and a boot, between a chair and a
        stool, between a book and a magazine. The same necessity to resort
        to examples will become even clearer when they define abstract
        terms.
2.   You may assign a single vague or ambiguous term, on which there is
        sure to be disagreement, for an extended discussion by each member
        of the class: success; the good life; normal sexuality; maturity;
        heroism; necessities, comforts, and luxuries.
            Some or all of the completed papers may be duplicated and dis-
        tributed to the whole class. Through a discussion or written as-
        signment the class may examine the criteria governing the different
        definitions. Can we reach a consensus? Why or why not? What are
        the implications of success or failure in reaching consensus about
        these particular terms?
3.   I ask students to tackle the definitions of words that have ac-
        quired several, sometimes contradictory, meanings. Example: dis-
        crimination. For most students, this word carries a negative con-
        notation. I sometimes offer the following example:

            A young woman who knows nothing about the mechanics of a car
            finds herself stranded in a parking lot because the engine
            of her car will not start. Passing near her are two people--
            a young man and a young woman. The car owner ignores the

10

young woman and turns to the young man, asking him if he can
identify and perhaps solve the problem of the stalled car.

Does this action represent "discrimination" in the negative sense?
Students must explain their answers in such a way as to make clear
how they define the term.
They might also be directed to examine the use of the word in
aesthetic criticism. Why has the word taken on negative connotations in other areas of discourse?
4.   Students can find examples of implicit definitions even in their
popular songs. Example: Pink Floyd in The Wall: "We don't need
no education. We don't need no thought control. . . . Teachers,
leave us kids alone." How is education defined in this song?

Readings in the Anthology

(For comments on the use of these essays, please see the discussions for
the anthology in this manual.)

"It's Failure, Not Success"
"Stereotype Truth"
"A Proposal to Abolish Grading"
        definition of education
"Drugs"
        definition of freedom
"Politics and the English Language"
        definition of political terms

Chapter 4

SUPPORT

FACTS AND INFERENCES

1.   Ask students to create a set of facts, then request that their
classmates derive inferences about the actions or people involved.
Examples: the contents of a grocery cart in the checkout line; an
accident; a crime.
2.   Assign reading of the following passage. Ask students to write
either a short or a long essay that summarizes some of the inferences we draw from observing what people wear. Since the subject
is so large (this excerpt is part of a book about clothing), this
exercise gives students practice in narrowing the subject of discussion and choosing a thesis statement or paragraph that can be
adequately developed in the number of words assigned.

11

> For thousands of years human beings have communicated with one another first in the language of dress. Long before I am near enough to talk to you on the street, in a meeting, or at a party, you announce your sex, age, and class to me through what you are wearing--and very possibly give me important information (or misinformation) as to your occupation, origin, personality, opinions, tastes, sexual desires and current mood. I may not be able to put what I observe into words, but I register the information unconsciously, and you simultaneously do the same for me.
>
> By the time we meet and converse we have already spoken to each other in an older and more universal tongue.
>
> The Language of Clothing, by Alison Lurie

3. On March 19, 1974, the New York Times published a long news account entitled "Death of a Black in a White Bar: Two Versions." This report of the death of a black man by a white off-duty policeman offers students, like the members of a jury, an outstanding opportunity to evaluate the conflicting data surrounding the killing as well as external evidence about the characters and history of the principals.

    A written assignment on this story calls for a clear thesis statement or paragraph, extraction of the most important data, and arrangement of materials in an orderly and emphatic way. Above all, it calls for an acknowledgement of the distinctions between facts and inferences in the testimony reported in the article and in the students' interpretations of the testimony. Not least, the students find this assignment interesting and provocative.

4. Ask students to look up information by advocates on both sides of the controversies surrounding one of the popular natural mysteries: the Loch Ness monster, the Bermuda Triangle, Findhorn, Bigfoot or Sasquatch, etc. Then assign a paper, short or long, that reviews the data on both sides and tries to come to a conclusion regarding the validity of the respective claims. Have students justify their conclusions by defending the evidence. If students find that they cannot make up their minds, this is also a conclusion, but they should be prepared to say why the evidence on both sides proved equally strong or equally weak.

5. An assignment with the same objectives but requiring no research can be based on the materials in another article from the New York Times (October 31, 1973), "Yeti-Like Monster Gives Staid Town in Illinois a Fright." Here students must evaluate factual evidence and consider carefully the reasons that such observations as those described in the article may not be trustworthy.

EVIDENCE

1.   From the first paper students have been required to use evidence.
        Having now read the more elaborate explanations of both factual and
        opinion evidence in Chapter 4, students can return to their claims
        of fact, value, and policy and reevaluate the facts and opinions
        in their essays. Would more data strengthen their claim? If so,
        what kind? Where can it be found? Would additional expert opinion
        make their arguments more convincing? If so, whose opinions?
        Where can they be found?
            If the students show some interest in revising their papers
        to include more data, encourage them to do so.

2.   A popular exercise calls on students to look up the New York Times
        edition that appeared on their birthdays and write a paper that
        emphasizes straightforward presentation of data to support their
        claims. Students must find a thesis around which the information
        can be organized--about the kinds of films being shown, the nature
        of women's fashions, advertisements for jobs, scientific discover-
        ies of the day, crimes, etc.

3.   Advertisements again. This time students choose ads that offer in-
        formation about the products. They then evaluate the data. In
        some cases, of course, they will be unequipped to decide whether
        the data are accurate or sufficient, but if the ads are directed
        to a lay audience, readers have a right to ask questions about the
        sufficiency, relevance, and recency of the data. In other words,
        if readers think that evidence for the virtues of the product is
        inadequate, what else would they want to know?

4.   Students sometimes approach the subject of information in ads with
        the preconception that ads do not offer information--only slogans.
        Students may therefore be asked to contrast two or more ads that
        offer different amounts and qualities of information. Is informa-
        tion more important in some kinds of ads than others--for example,
        in car ads, which are often dense with facts?

5.   If there is time for lengthier papers, ask students to examine the
        evidence in the following cases (or any others that remain contro-
        versial):
        (a)   assassination of President John F. Kennedy, 1963
        (b)   the kidnapping of Patty Hearst, 1974
        (c)   the kidnapping and murder of the Lindbergh baby, 1932
        (d)   the Sacco-Vanzetti case, 1927

6.   In leading students to examine the credentials of experts, ask them
        to consider the authors in the text and anthology as "experts." It
        will be easy enough to identify such writers as Lewis Thomas and
        Ruth Hubbard--both respected scientists--as authorities in their
        fields. Even in more problematic disciplines, such as political
        science, we recognize the authority of Walter Lippmann, for exam-
        ple, who spent a lifetime studying government and earned the ap-
        proval of other political scientists.

But what are we to say of writers who reflect on their personal experience or expound their philosophies? Why do we think Ellen Goodman's views worth reading? After all, she is probably no more an "expert" on failure and success than any of her readers.

It might come as a small revelation to students, and pertinent to their participation in a writing course, to recognize that the credibility of Goodman and other nonprofessional "experts" is based largely on their excellence as writers. They can discover interesting propositions, and organize, develop, and express them in spirited and highly readable prose. They are intelligent, of course, but also curious about most subjects and well informed about many. Students might speculate on the kinds of social phenomena that such writers as Ellen Goodman, John Leo, Gloria Steinem, Noel Perrin (an English teacher who often writes outside his field), and Gore Vidal have examined and become knowledgeable about in order to write the particular essays that appear in the Anthology and Opposing Viewpoints.

STATISTICS

1. Students usually need practice in reporting statistics--extracting them from news stories and arranging them in interesting and readable form. Students can research the following subjects and report the information as data that might support a claim. They should, of course, limit the time period for the data. Have them submit their prose summaries to their classmates. Are the data clear and accessible to these readers?
   (a) world population growth
   (b) teenage pregnancies
   (c) women in the labor market
   (d) growth of ethnic populations in the U.S.
   (e) American marriage patterns
   (f) dimensions of poverty
   (g) voting patterns in the 1984 elections
2. The two books mentioned below are entertaining and informative references for both teachers and students. They are full of useful examples that should help students avoid some of the common pitfalls in interpreting and reporting statistical evidence.

   Stephen K. Campbell, Flaws and Fallacies in Statistical Thinking (Englewood Cliffs, N.J.: Prentice-Hall, Inc., 1974).
   Darrell Huff, How to Lie with Statistics (New York: W.W. Norton, 1954).

3. Some students may be interested in and sufficiently informed about polling techniques to evaluate some of the famous polling gaffes: the Literary Digest poll of 1936 that predicted that Alfred Landon would defeat Franklin D. Roosevelt or the 1948 Gallup Poll that

predicted Dewey would defeat Truman. Students might want to pre-
dict the reasons such mistakes probably will not recur.

APPEALS TO NEEDS AND VALUES

1.   A lively and immediate source of appeals to needs and values is
      found in speeches--students may be directed to Vital Speeches of
      the Day, which publishes speeches from a variety of speechmakers.
            In the anthology of this book, the speech of Martin Luther
      King, Jr., "I Have a Dream," is an outstanding example of spoken
      discourse that makes a profoundly emotional appeal. Other famous
      speeches for the purposes of this unit include:
      (a)   Clarence Darrow's "Address to the Prisoners of Cook County
             Jail" in 1902
      (b)   then Vice-President Richard Nixon's "Checkers" speech in
             1952
      (c)   President John F. Kennedy's Inaugural Address in 1960
      (d)   Senator Edward Kennedy's TV address explaining to the
             people of Massachusetts his behavior during and after the
             accident at Chappaquiddick in 1969.
            For example, Darrow's speech is remarkable for the inconsis-
      tency of his argument and its numerous fallacies, both of which
      have been overlooked by textbooks that reprint the address. Edward
      Kennedy's speech makes a personal appeal, arousing sympathy for his
      suffering and inducing guilt in the listener for having accused him
      unjustly.
            A more recent group of speeches--Basic Speeches, delivered by
      the candidates for the Presidency in 1984--was printed by the New
      York Times during the year. The first group, published in summer
      1984, included the speeches of all the major Democratic candidates:
      Mondale, Hart, Glenn, McGovern, and Jackson--as well as those of
      President Reagan. A second group, published in fall 1984, included
      the basic speeches of Reagan, Bush, Mondale, and Ferraro. All of
      the speeches were excellent compendiums of the values on which
      their candidacies were based.
2.   Advertisements by large corporations (Mobil, United Technologies,
      Exxon) appearing frequently in newspapers and magazines comment on
      political and social issues rather than the merits of their prod-
      ucts. As short essays they can be useful for examination of values
      based on what is perceived to be common consent.
      (a)   What values do the advertisers assume that we share?
      (b)   What evidence (examples, facts, statistics) do they offer
             to persuade the reader that their proposals will support
             our values?
      (c)   What is the tone of the essay (reasonable, generous, angry,
             sarcastic, humorous)?
3.   Also useful are the ads that promise power, riches, great beauty,

(text pages 108-131)

etc. Many of the most outrageous ones appear in <u>The National Enquirer</u> and other gossip sheets.
- (a)   Can you infer to what audience they make a strong appeal?
- (b)   What fears, needs, desires, do these appeal to?
- (c)   What attempts are made to provide credibility?

<u>Readings</u> <u>in</u> <u>the</u> <u>Anthology</u>

(For comments on the use of these essays, please see the discussions for the anthology in this manual.)
    Since support is integral to any argument, all the selections in the anthology will provide examples of different kinds of support. The following essays, however, are strong in particular strategies that students can discover without much difficulty.

"The Ignored Lesson of Anne Frank"
    historical evidence; appeals to the values of courage, willingness to face the truth about evil
"Where College Fails Us"
    statistics; other factual data; appeals to values of thrift, honesty, independence
"Stereotype Truth"
    historical evidence
"Test-Tube Babies: Solution or Problem?"
    medical evidence; appeals to values of liberal feminism, social justice
"Homosexuality: Tolerance Versus Approval"
    historical evidence; factual evidence to refute popular assumptions; appeals to values governing choices in a free society
"Politics and the English Language"
    historical evidence; examples of language; appeals to love of truth, hatred of tyranny
"A Modest Proposal"
    historical evidence; statistics (although used ironically); appeals to compassion and justice
"The Health-Care System"
    medical data

Chapter 5

WARRANTS

1.   Although the definition of the warrant in <u>The</u> <u>Uses</u> <u>of</u> <u>Argument</u> is more complicated than we have made it appear, for the purposes of a freshman composition course, those of us who have used the

Toulmin model with some success believe that the model works best
if we define the warrant as synonymous with assumption, a belief we
take for granted, or a general principle underlying other beliefs
and attitudes. If students raise questions, we can always widen
the definition.

    For obvious reasons the concept of the warrant is more diffi-
cult for students to assimilate than that of support, in part because they have seldom been required to make their assumptions explicit. Fortunately for teaching purposes, the examples that we
can use are so numerous and so varied that we may call attention to
the warrant repeatedly without losing student interest.

2.   Advertisements offer a rich and accessible source of material.
Choose the ads yourself (I keep a file of provocative advertisements), especially those in which the warrant is unexpressed. Example: "Boodles: The Most Expensive Gin in the World."

    Or students may select their own ads and write out the war-
rants, either implicit or explicit. Then the student or the whole
class may decide on the validity of the argument based on the particular warrant underlying the advertiser's claim.

3.   Subjects for examination of warrants appear almost every day in
school newspapers. Sometimes the subjects are about education or
other matters relevant to the function and management of the
school; sometimes they respond to the world outside. Below are
some current issues on my own campus:

    (a)   A proposal to introduce a core requirement for cultivating
          knowledge and awareness of Third World cultures. (What as-
          sumptions about education have prompted this proposal?)

    (b)   A motion in the student Senate to suspend funding of con-
          troversial student groups on campus, among them religious
          groups and the Gay Alliance. (What assumptions about the
          relationship between taxation and social purpose should
          govern here?)

    (c)   Beauty pageants. (What assumptions about sex and beauty
          cause feminists to attack them?)

    (d)   The appearance of the Dalai Lama on campus. (What assump-
          tions about Eastern religions underlie their present-day
          attraction for some young people?)

4.   Other sources for analysis of warrants:

    (a)   Etiquette books. An interesting assignment would compare
          etiquette books of a generation or more ago with contem-
          porary ones. Have there been large changes? Small
          changes? In what areas? On what assumptions about social
          relationships and freedom have these changes been based?

    (b)   Advice columns in newspapers and magazines. What assump-
          tions about marriage, sexual problems, child rearing, re-
          ligion, etc. underlie the advice of the columnists?

    (c)   Magazines for teenagers. Have they changed in the last
          fifteen or twenty years? On what assumptions about the

lives and values of teenagers have the publishers based their changes?

5.   Go back to the earlier papers of definition and defense of value and policy claims and examine the warrants, expressed or unexpressed. Example: In defending his decision never to marry, a student writes that he values his freedom. What does he assume about marriage, love, individuality, commitment, etc.?

6.   Students enjoy the familiar game in which a disaster has left a small number of people alive, and the players must choose an even smaller number to survive. The choices of the players reflect their assumptions about an ideal world. Whenever classes engage in this exercise, they discover how difficult it is for even a class of twenty fairly similar students to arrive at a consensus. Of course, the players must defend their selection of particular people and the order in which they rank them.

"Who Should Survive?"

Task: Choose seven people to survive. List them in the order in which you would choose them and indicate the reasons for your selection, i.e., why you chose these particular persons and why you placed them in this particular order.

PEOPLE:

1.   Dr. Dane--thirty-seven, white, no religious affiliation, Ph.D. in history, college professor, in good health (jogs daily), hobby is botany, enjoys politics, married with one child (Bobby).

2.   Mrs. Dane--thirty-eight, white, Jewish, rather obese, diabetic, M.A. in psychology, counselor in a mental health clinic, married to Dr. Dane, has one child.

3.   Bobby Dane--ten, white, Jewish, mentally retarded with IQ of 70, healthy and strong for his age.

4.   Mrs. Garcia--twenty-three, Spanish-American, Catholic, ninth-grade education, cocktail waitress, worked as a prostitute, married at age sixteen, divorced at age eighteen, has one child (Jean) whom she refuses to leave behind.

5.   Jean Garcia--three months old, Spanish-American, healthy.

6.   Mary Evans--eighteen, black, Protestant, trade school education, wears glasses, artistic.

7.   Mr. Newton--twenty-five, black power advocate, starting last year of medical school, suspected homosexual activity, music as a hobby, physical fitness nut.

8.   Mrs. Clark--twenty-eight, black, Protestant, daughter of a minister, college graduate, electronics engineer, single now after a brief marriage, member of Zero Population Growth, loves to tinker and has a mechanical mind.

9.   Mr. Blake--fifty-one, white, Mormon, B.S. in mechanics,

married with four children, enjoys outdoors, much experience in construction, quite handy, sympathizes with anti-
black views.
10.   Father Frans--thirty-seven, white, Catholic, priest, active
in civil rights, former college athlete, farming background,
often criticized for liberal views.
11.   Dr. Gonzales--sixty-six, Spanish-American, Catholic, doctor
in general practice, two heart attacks in the past five
years, loves literature and quotes extensively.

Readings in the Anthology

(For comments on the use of these essays, please see the discussions for
the anthology in this manual.)
    Since warrants are inherent in all arguments, all the selections in
the anthology will offer opportunities for students to recognize and evaluate them. In the following essays, however, warrants are relatively easy
to discover.

"A Proposal to Abolish Grading"
    the nature and purpose of education
"I Have a Dream"
    the possibilities of human nature and social progress
"Homosexuality: Tolerance Versus Approval"
    refutation of common assumptions about homosexuality; rights in a
democracy
"The Case for Torture"
    the limits of freedom; the smaller versus the larger good; the rights
of people to defend themselves
"The Indispensable Opposition"
    the foundations of democracy; tolerance versus necessity; the way to
discover truth
"The Penalty of Death"
    human nature; the rights of a moral society
"The War of the Woods"
    class conflict in recreational activities
"Socrates to His Accusers"
    the good life; the virtuous citizen
"Politics and the English Language"
    the relationship between political speech and action and the use of
language

Chapter 6

LANGUAGE

1.   Again we turn to advertisements for their use of slogans, clichés, and emotive language. Advertising claims in airline ads, we are told by a national advertising group, "promise great buys and then dissolve into airline jargon filled with restrictions." Ask students to examine some airline ads for jargon and code words that are meaningless or slippery.

    A paperback entitled I Can Sell You Anything by Carl P. Wrighter (Ballantine, 1972) offers a popular attack on techniques of advertising. Wrighter supports his claims by offering dozens of examples of "weasel words" in specific commercial advertisements. The claims of each ad are clearly stated. Often the argument is exaggerated, and some of the ads will no longer be familiar to students, but they can use Wrighter's formulas as a model, choosing their own ads and substituting their own weasel words.

2.   Have students collect literature from various politically active groups on campus. Assign a study of the language based on some of the categories in the text: connotations, euphemisms, clichés, slogans, slanted language, picturesque language.

    (a)   Is the message persuasive? How much of the persuasive effect is due to the way that language is used?

    (b)   Identify terms that you consider effective and tell why.

    (c)   Identify terms that you consider ineffective and tell why.

3.   Students can find slogans everywhere. The slogans will, of course, differ from year to year and from place to place, depending on the emergence of new issues. In 1984, an election year, some slogans were generated, though not so many as we might have expected. Ask students to compose their own political slogans and defend them. To whom does the slogan appeal? What shortcuts have been taken, that is, what questions about your abbreviated argument might be asked by an unfriendly reader?

4.   Although slogans were scarce, there were plenty of clichés--statements of obvious ideas. Students can examine the Basic Speeches referred to in assignments for Chapter 4. They might consider answers to the following questions: Can the use of clichés be justified? What would be the effect of substituting unusual ideas, even a surprising and perhaps unpleasant truth?

5.   Have students examine some of the classic speeches of the past: Patrick Henry's Speech Before the Virginia Convention of 1775, Lincoln's Gettysburg Address, Winston Churchill's address to the

Congress of the United States of America on December 26, 1941.
Students will notice that all of these speeches contain memorable
phrases. Ask whether they think that the language in these
speeches differs in any significant way from the language of the
Basic Speeches of 1984. Have them explain any differences and describe how they contribute to the success or failure of particular
speeches.

6. Students might try writing their own high school commencement ad-
    dresses, avoiding both the clichés of Woody Allen and the bitter
    invective of Jacob Neusner.

7. I have used an excerpt describing the actions of Henry VIII to dem-
    onstrate the use of partisan language by a Catholic historian. Be-
    low is a passage from a Protestant historian, G. M. Trevelyan,
    about the same events of the English Reformation but exhibiting,
    through the use of selective language, an entirely different point
    of view. Students may be asked to pick out the words and phrases
    that indicate slanting.

> It is often falsely asserted that the [Protestant] Refor-
> mation was a plunder of the poor; that it dispossessed them of
> their heritage in favor of a squirearchy [landed proprietor
> class]. The fact is that the medieval Church, on its finan-
> cial side, was a squirearchy richer and more jealous of its
> possessions than any which had existed since the Reformation.
> What the revolution did was to transfer enormous wealth from
> one squirearchy to another; from a squirearchy which, in its
> very nature, was intensely conservative and seldom let go of
> anything in its possessions, to another which lived far more
> among the people, and whose extravagances often led to the
> division of the land, so that there grew up in Elizabethan
> and Jacobean times a whole class of small yeoman farmers.
>
> The medieval Church was, no doubt, more friendly to the
> poor than any State Institution of those days would have been.
> But it was far from that Christian fraternity and generous
> beneficence which is often claimed for it, and which the ear-
> liest Christianity had actually displayed. It was deeply
> feudalized; it was no longer a really democratic institution
> in any strict sense of the word. Popes were the most absolute
> sovereigns of their day, and sometimes the most luxurious and
> most directly responsible for those wars which were chronic
> in Christendom.

I have tried to encourage students to uncover other examples in
their own texts, but they find this difficult to do. The exercise
above will at least induce a healthy caution about the objectivity
of textbook writers, even distinguished historians.

21

(text pages 173-194)

<u>Readings</u> <u>in</u> <u>the</u> <u>Anthology</u>

(For comments on the use of these essays, please see the discussions for
the anthology in this manual.)

"I Have a Dream"
"Politics and the English Language"
"A Modest Proposal"

Chapter 7

INDUCTION, DEDUCTION, AND LOGICAL FALLACIES

1.   I have expressed elsewhere my reluctance to use exercises in induc-
      tion and deduction. Because they have only a tenuous connection
      with the actual process of composing an argument, we may spend our
      limited time more profitably in attention to the other elements of
      argument.
2.   The teaching of fallacies poses special, though not insuperable,
      problems. Some fallacious statements by public figures are obvi-
      ous, like those in the list of exercises in the text. But argu-
      ments by professional writers often contain concealed fallacies or
      fallacies that uninformed students are unable to identify. I have
      remarked on what I consider to be faulty reasoning in speeches and
      articles by Clarence Darrow--in fact, I am surprised at the gener-
      osity accorded by editors to some clearly deficient arguments. One
      example that comes immediately to mind is Ashley Montagu's "Man,
      the Ignoble Savage?" (from <u>The</u> <u>Nature</u> <u>of</u> <u>Human</u> <u>Aggression</u>). This
      essay, reprinted in several readers, purports to be an attack on
      the use of examples by others, but Montagu offers only one example
      in rebuttal, and this example is a scarcely credible rumor that
      remains unsubstantiated. (An interesting assignment would be to
      ask students to look for more convincing research to support Monta-
      gu's claim.)
          The rule for all of us, I think--teachers and students alike--
      is to cultivate fearlessness in our criticism of articles by puta-
      tive experts. Since freshman students are naturally disinclined
      to be critical of their mentors (publicly, at least), we may risk
      overzealousness in uncovering faulty arguments in textbooks, news-
      papers, and magazines. Advertisers are not the only arguers guilty
      of concealment or distorted reasoning.
3.   I ask students to be on the alert for dubious arguments in what
      they read and hear and to bring them in for examination by the
      class. If they are keeping journals, they may record these falla-
      cies or what they interpret as fallacies in their journals. The

nomenclature is not important. Some of their entries will turn out to be examples of sound reasoning after all, but no matter. The objective of the exercise is increased alertness. Sensitive discrimination will, we hope, come later.

In some cases, students will be lucky to find explicit references to fallacies, as in the beginning of this letter (Wall Street Journal, November 15, 1983): "Your editorial is an illustration of the slippery slope argument." Less explicitly, the writer will say (Wall Street Journal, December 7, 1983): "Your editorial was critical of Surgeon General C. Everett Koop for 'citing particularly egregious magazine articles and medical cases as proof that the U.S. could easily slip into some Nazi-like approval of general euthanasia.' I, for one, would not dismiss Dr. Koop's concern quite so readily."

4. In my experience at half a dozen campuses, school newspapers are rife with weak and fallacious arguments in the editorials and letters to the editor. As a source of fallacies, they have two advantages: They are easily available, and students probably feel fewer inhibitions in attacking their peers.

PART TWO

OPPOSING VIEWPOINTS

Introduction

1. The debates, articles, and letters in this section represent the argumentative process in its clearest and most understandable form. If throughout the semester we have emphasized that arguments are dialogues, the selections given here will show students how the dialogues work, that is, how people on opposing sides actually respond to each other, whether well or poorly. Where it is clear that the response is not direct, that there is no clash, the debates can be equally instructive.

2. Opposing Viewpoints may be used as a discrete unit or as a source of materials for assignments in the text.

    (a) If it is used as a self-contained unit, the introduction and the questions that precede it suggest a number of ways of examining the material and writing about it. The debate instructions that follow give, I hope, sufficient details for the organization of a classroom debate, oral or written.

    (b) Opposing Viewpoints also lends itself for use as a source of data, expert opinion, motivational appeals, warrants, and ethical and unethical use of language. In fulfilling assignments that call for supporting materials students may find material here, either as a substitute for or in addition to library research. In several places in the manual I have suggested assignments that give students the opportunity to look for support for their claims among the selections in Opposing Viewpoints.

3. Some of these subjects will be more effective than others for a given group of students, depending on their experiences and knowledge of and involvement with the subject. Immigration Policy, for example, may be more significant for students in areas of the country where immigrants have made a visible impact. Euthanasia may

strike a chord in a place where the fate of a handicapped infant is being publicly debated.

When time does not permit use of all the subjects, I choose the most provocative ones, those that will produce, as far as I can tell, the liveliest feelings, both for and against.

4. Given the timeliness of these subjects, new data will be indispensable to any evaluation. This means research to discover whether the facts have changed since the articles and letters in the text were written. What is the present state of the Simpson-Mazzoli bill on immigration? What has happened to bills being introduced in several cities that define pornography as a violation of women's civil rights? What legal measures are being taken that affect experimentation with animals? Once new data have been uncovered, students may want to argue about the effects, predicting whether conditions will be better or worse as a result of changes.

5. Debate I seldom assign long research papers in freshman classes. I have found that the problems--students' lack of time, their difficulty in finding a defensible thesis, the risks of plagiarism--outweigh the benefits.

However, an enormously productive unit may be organized around formal classroom debate. Although debate is almost always an oral exercise, there is plenty of opportunity in a writing class for students to commit their outlines to paper, develop major points that cannot be adequately treated in the five minutes allotted to oral presentation, and make extended critiques of the debates of their classmates.

Each debate usually requires four people, two on the affirmative side, two on the negative, although the Lincoln-Douglass format--one debater on each side--is also possible. If time does not permit a round of formal debates, the class may choose four or five debate subjects, and each team produce an argument that will be duplicated or read aloud for consideration by the whole class. This organization reduces the arguments to one on each side and eliminates rebuttal time. After reading or hearing the arguments, the class may write evaluations based on answers to the questions on the Debate sheet.

For supporting materials students should confine themselves to the data in this section. Their efforts will involve extracting the relevant issues and organizing them in a succinct and understandable way. They may also, of course, need to do further research for more recent data.

DEBATE

Debate may be considered an extension of the problem-solving analysis. The debaters are considering the merits of a solution to some problem, for example, a plan to restrict government agencies in their investigations of private citizens.

The debate proposition is always a two-sided question, that is, it can be answered yes or no.

The proposition is worded so that the affirmative (yes) side will be arguing for a change in policy, or, in the case of value questions, a new idea. (The argument that violence is justified in civil rights cases is an example of the latter.) Because the affirmative is arguing for a change, they are said to have the burden of proof, while the negative has only to defend the status quo.

The affirmative argument usually centers around three stock issues that grow out of the problem-solving analysis. The affirmative will argue:

1. that there is a need for a change.
2. that their proposal will meet the need.
3. that their proposal is the best solution to the problem. These stock issues are referred to as need, plan, and advantages.

The negative may answer the affirmative case in a number of ways.

1. They may debate every issue. "There is no problem, and even if there were your plan is expensive, inefficient, and undesirable."
2. They may waive an issue. "Yes, indeed, we agree there is a serious problem, but your proposed solution is useless."
3. They may propose a counterplan. "Things are bad all right, but I have a better idea for improving them than yours." Tournament debaters do not do this too often for strategic reasons: it means the negative must assume part of the burden of proof.

Following are some questions you might consider as you listen to a debate:

1. How important is definition of terms? Does it become an issue in the debate?
2. Does the negative attack the affirmative argument on every point or does the debate narrow to one or two issues?
3. Do the speakers base their arguments on any generally accepted principles or values, such as justice, individual freedom, constitutional guarantees?
4. Do you find examples of causal argument, argument from example, or argument from analogy?
5. How important is evidence in the debate? Do the speakers question the credibility of each other's sources? To what extent, if any, does the argument center around evidence?
6. What comments would you make on the speakers' oral presentation (delivery)?
7. Which side do you think won, and why?

ADDITIONAL ISSUES

Chapter 1

AFFIRMATIVE ACTION

Having responded to the discussion questions at the end of the section, students might turn to the following questions:

1. How did the Democratic and Republican platforms in 1984 treat affirmative action? Were the differences substantial, based on different assumptions about opportunity, fairness, incentive, freedom, etc.? (An interesting and instructive lesson in the significance of punctuation emerged during the internal platform debates.)

> DALLAS, Aug. 14--The proposed tax statement for the Republican platform, before amendment, read:
> "We therefore oppose any attempt to increase taxes which would harm the recovery and reverse the trend toward restoring control of the economy to individual Americans."
> The statement, as amended to meet conservatives' objections, reads:
> "We therefore oppose any attempt to increase taxes, which would harm the recovery and reverse the trend toward restoring control of the economy to individual Americans."
> Originally, Mr. Jackson tried to add this language to the Democratic platform plank on affirmative action: "The Democratic Party opposes quotas which are inconsistent with the principles of our country." This was rejected by Walter F. Mondale's forces for wont of a comma after the word "quotas." Mr. Mondale wanted it clear that all quotas were bad.
>
> New York Times
> August 14, 1984

2. Should employers of professional athletic teams, symphony orchestras, theatrical companies, etc., be forced by law to observe quotas for minority members? Is there a difference between these quotas and quotas for employment in industry or admission to college? Explain.

3. Affirmative action is usually regarded from the point of view of those who will be directly benefited--that is, those who will be hired by an employer or admitted to a school. If we look at affirmative action from the point of view of certain groups outside--

those who will be served by the beneficiary--do we see a different perspective? Provide support for your answer.
4. Affirmative action, which began with an attempt to redress the grievances of racial minorities who had been massively discriminated against in the past, has now been extended to rights of employment for the elderly, the handicapped, the mentally retarded, the alcoholic, etc. Comment on this development.

Reference: The United States Commission on Civil Rights (Washington, D.C. 20425) issues statements from time to time on its own decisions and those of the Courts on questions related to civil rights, including affirmative action.

Chapter 2

ANIMAL RIGHTS

1. The debate continues to widen in unexpected ways. Late in October 1984 the heart of a young baboon was transplanted into the body of a human infant, Baby Fae, who would otherwise not have survived beyond two weeks. On November 16 Baby Fae died of kidney failure. Demonstrators outside the hospital had protested against the sacrifice of a healthy animal to prolong the life of a sick human being. Several other transplants of animal organs into human bodies are planned. Does this portend the eventual breeding of animals to be killed for their organs--as we breed animals for food? What response should we make to this new development? Students will need to consult newspapers and magazines for the history of the case of Baby Fae and the debate it generated among physicians, clergy, and the public.
2. On some campuses academic departments maintain laboratories that use animals for experimentation. Ask students to interview those responsible for the experiments and to write an evaluative report that discusses the nature of the experiments and the justification for them.
3. The adoption of vegetarianism, at least partly for ethical reasons, is growing on our campus and therefore, I suspect, on others as well. Students in the class who are ethical vegetarians may examine their own advance toward this practice and defend it against the arguments of meat-eaters.

31

Chapter 3

EUTHANASIA

1. Hardly a week passes that the media do not report a case in which
    death for a terminally ill or severely disabled person is being
    debated by the family, the physicians, or the state. Students are
    sometimes able to contribute experiences about such patients in
    their own families. An assignment requires them to select a recent
    case, one still undecided, and come to a decision about the proper
    treatment, basing their argument on some of the assumptions raised
    by the writers in this section.
2. Some students who have an interest in and understanding of the
    technology may want to describe the different kinds of machines
    and drugs now used to keep people alive and to evaluate their ef-
    fectiveness and desirability.
3. If suicide is acceptable for the elderly whose lives have become
    intolerable as a result of illness, why is it unacceptable for
    young people who are not ill but who also find it impossible to go
    on living?
4. Hospitals around the country are beginning to establish ethics
    committees to deal with the problems raised by the new medical
    technologies. An article in the New York Times, November 4, 1984,
    describes the growth of these committees and the difficult deci-
    sions they face.
        If a hospital, medical school, or philosophy department in
    your school--or another easily accessible facility--has established
    an ethics committee or a course that revolves around problems of
    euthanasia, students may interview one or more of the people con-
    nected with the committee or course and analyze the issues that
    emerge.

Chapter 4

IMMIGRATION POLICY

1. Some students whose immigrant roots are still fresh may be invited
    to offer a personal perspective, to explain why they and their
    families chose to come to America, what their resources were, what

they expected to find, whether their expectations have been satisfied. They should include a summary of the immigration laws that
enabled them to enter the country when they did. The class may respond to the presentation, whether oral or written, in writing,
answering such questions as: Should the immigration laws be more
liberal? Does the knowledge of a personal experience influence
your answer? What seem to be the primary motives for leaving a
native country? What are the greatest difficulties that the immigrant encounters in the new country? Are the difficulties different for different immigrants? What policies should be adopted
to make things easier?

2. The experience of the present generation of immigrants may be com-
pared--and contrasted--to that of an earlier generation, especially
the great movement from southern and eastern Europe at the turn of
the century. Numberless articles, books, movies, and plays describe and celebrate this seminal experience.

In 1969 Arno Press, a Publishing and Library Service of the
New York Times, republished the forty-two-volume American Immigration Collection, basic reference materials on American immigration
"especially useful for the story of the immigrant in American history and of minority groups in the U.S."

If your school or a nearby library contains this collection,
students will have access to an invaluable resource for research
into the backgrounds of every immigrant group from the middle of
the nineteenth century.

Oscar Handlin's The Uprooted (1952), subtitled The Epic Story
of the Great Migrations that Made the American People, is an exceptionally readable account. In his Acknowledgements Handlin
lists books by and about immigrants that he found enlightening.

Chapter 5

PORNOGRAPHY

1. On many campuses the debate between free access to pornographic
materials and the dangers it may pose to some members of the com-
munity has broken out over specific issues. In our school two
battles have been fought in recent years--over the right of a group
to show X-rated films on campus and over the right of the Campus
Store to sell Penthouse, Playgirl, and Hustler.

Whether such specific conflicts have emerged on your campus,
hypothetical examples will work equally well to provoke discussion
on both sides of the issues. Students will discover that the
larger issues of freedom and civil rights are difficult if not im-
possible to understand unless they are brought down to actual cases.

33

(text pages 293-329)

2.   I have found it fruitful to ask advocates of opposing positions, usually members of partisan groups on campus, to address the class. The class then evaluates the arguments, using a set of criteria on which we have agreed beforehand.

3.   Vanessa Williams, Miss America of 1983, was stripped of her crown when it was discovered that she had posed for _Hustler_ in photographs described as pornographic. Do students agree that her punishment was justified, that Williams had engaged in an activity that reflected unfavorably on the role model she was expected to provide as Miss America? Some defenders of Williams suggest that the Miss America contest itself contains pornographic elements.

PART THREE

ANTHOLOGY

Introduction

"Reading requires more than words."[1] This observation serves as a partial text for the comments that follow on the use of the anthology. To understand and enjoy the selections in the anthology, students will need not only the ability to decode the linguistic symbols but informa-tion--about historical events and current social phenomena. Even where the necessary information appears in the essay, the authors will assume a certain degree of literary sophistication in connecting one set of data with another.

There are two sources for the background information and the inter-pretation of that information: the library and the instructor. Use of the library needs no recommendation from me, but I should like to put in a word for the instructor as a resource. Notwithstanding the prevailing distaste for lecturing in composition courses, it seems to me perfectly legitimate for instructors to give students the information they need in a short summary before they proceed, and even to interpret the data if necessary, whenever such an introduction saves valuable time, enlivens the information, and arouses student interest as library research often does not.

Since each selection in the anthology is followed by questions and writing suggestions, I have offered here only occasional questions and suggestions for classroom activities. Instead I have written about these essays largely as I myself have responded to them--sometimes in full agreement, sometimes in partial acquiescence--and as I have discussed them with students, who have often disagreed with me.

---

1. E. D. Hirsch, Jr., "Reading Requires More than Words," The New York Times Education Survey, November 12, 1984, p. 65.

Bruno Bettelheim, "The Ignored Lesson of Anne Frank" (p. 333)

Most students will have a general familiarity with the Holocaust. They may need to be informed, however, about the SS, Nazi racial ideology, the actual purpose and functioning of concentration camps, the definition of "Aryan" as used by the Nazis, pogroms, even the location of places mentioned in the essay. Some students in the class may be sufficiently knowledgeable to give a summary of these events and ideas. In addition, in the last paragraph Bettelheim introduces a reference to Negroes in Africa and apartheid, which may also need explanation.

Bettelheim's essay is the expression of a severe value judgment. He excoriates not only the inertia and blindness that prevented people like the Franks from resisting their fate but, more importantly, the uncritical response of those who have derived the wrong lesson from the Franks' experience. Because the essay is long and contains ideas that may be difficult or unfamiliar, students should be directed to give special attention to the passages in which Bettelheim summarizes his claims: paragraph 3 on page 334, paragraph 16 on page 337, paragraph 18 on page 337, and the transitional last paragraph (19) on page 337, which relates the fate of the Franks to a larger problem, the refusal of many others to face the reality of Nazi terror.

The difficulty for students in understanding Bettelheim derives from the necessity to overcome a strong prejudice in favor of the response that Bettelheim attacks. If they are familiar with Anne Frank's story, they have learned to admire her; now they are asked to substitute for this warm, loving response a condemnation of people who suffered excruciatingly.

Throughout the essay Bettelheim supports his general statements with vivid stories from his own experience and his reading. As distinguished psychoanalyst and survivor of Buchenwald, he provides overwhelming authority for his explanations.

The headnote speaks of Bettelheim's bitterness. Ask students to find both direct and indirect expression of his feelings in his use of language. Does his bitterness reflect a lament for the needless destruction of hundreds of thousands, perhaps millions, of Jews because they behaved like the Franks? Or contempt for those who were too cowardly or too ignorant to consider the possibility of escape?

It is worth noting that in recent revisions of American history, some writers have emphasized the incidence of slave revolts in this country, as if to remind us that all slaves did not quietly accept their fate. Ask students to refer to the three psychological mechanisms mentioned at the beginning of Bettelheim's essay. Do they explain our attitudes toward American slaves, American Indians, Vietnamese boat people?

Caroline Bird, "Where College Fails Us" (p. 345)

Bird makes the factual claim that college does not serve the purposes of all the students who are enrolled. Her essay is a model of its kind, too long for students to imitate in its entirety, but rich in the elements of argument that students will examine in the text. It is strong in its use of evidence to support the claim: ample data in the form of examples and explanations, the effective use of statistics, especially in comparisons (e.g., between the number of jobs available and the number of graduates in a specific field), and attention to most of the significant issues concerning college attendance. The warrant is clear--that any institution serving only a minority (those who love to read, study, and write) should not be considered indispensable to the goals of the majority.

The values that Bird espouses also deserve comment: thrift, independence, honesty, courage. Ask students to find references to them, both implicit and explicit.

Students should have little difficulty with the material of this essay, which speaks directly to their own experience. They should examine all or most of the issues that Bird uncovers and evaluate them in the light of the knowledge they have so far acquired.

Ellen Goodman, "It's Failure, Not Success" (p. 355)

Goodman's essay is an outstanding example of an evaluative claim. Despite the familiar, sprightly style and the brevity of the piece, it may not be particularly easy for freshmen to grasp at first reading. Here is a case where some knowledge of the human-potential movement and of books offering advice on the acquisition of power and status will be necessary to an understanding of Goodman's criticism. To introduce students to these subjects, you might read to the class several paragraphs from one of Michael Korda's books or show some advertisements for similar books, with descriptions of their contents and extravagant praise from pseudoexperts and satisfied customers.

Having acquired this background, students will then need to confront Goodman's main point--that we should acknowledge our shortcomings and try to eradicate them instead of excusing and accepting them in the spirit of a self-satisfied tolerance, or using them to advance our own selfish interest. Tolerance has a comforting ring (in Russell Baker's words, it

39

makes us "feel terrific") and we relinquish it with some misgiving, especially if we are asked to be "judgmental."

Since Goodman dares to speak of "right" and "wrong," students may engage in a discussion of actions and attributes that deserve such characterizations. How do the students define "right" and "wrong"? Are there any absolutes? If so, what are they and why? If not, what principles underlie their rejection?

Paul Goodman, "A Proposal to Abolish Grading" (p. 358)

Information: From the context students can probably ascertain Goodman's point in describing the purpose of testing in medieval universities. In fact, the process will remind them of present-day examinations for admission to medical practice and the bar.

Goodman's claim may not be a popular one with students, who almost universally want to view grades as a scale on which to measure their standing and their progress. (I was told by a student who had attended a private school where grading was not prescribed that he and his fellow students awarded themselves letter grades on the basis of the teacher's comments on their papers.) Students may respect—in theory, at least— Goodman's view that students should take responsibility for their own learning, and they will agree that testing for grades is disagreeable, but they will ask not only how they are to interpret their test results if no comparisons are available but how, even without grades, students can be prevented from competing with one another. One has only to read about the discovery of the double helix to realize how fiercely dedicated and intelligent scholars can seek to advance themselves at the expense of their colleagues, without grades as a measure.

Goodman declines to tell whether he would evaluate students at all. Nor does he say how love of the subject itself can be fostered in students who arrive uninspired and undirected. Goodman's remedy is "to fire a do-nothing out of your class." Perhaps it is relevant to remember that Goodman himself made extraordinary efforts to educate himself, bicycling from New York to New Haven in order to attend classes and sitting in on classes in which he was not enrolled. (So the legend goes, anyway.) Does he have in mind only students like himself, of whom there can never have been a large number? Compare Meg Greenfield's essay in the text. She too argues for learning for its own sake but neglects to tell us how this is to be accomplished. Students may have good ideas of their own about ways to bring about such learning.

Interested students can find an abundance of material on testing and evaluation by educators and psychologists, some of whom take issue with Goodman's assumptions.

William Helmreich, "Stereotype Truth" (p. 362)

Helmreich defends what is probably the clearest and most straight-
forward factual claim in the anthology. For this reason it serves as an
excellent model for students. Even the length is appropriate. There is
an explicit thesis statement in the third paragraph and a neat transition,
"Let's take some examples," to the body of the essay. The examples--His-
panics, Jews, and blacks--will be familiar to most students, if not
through personal experience, through reading, television, and movies.
Students should concentrate on Helmreich's use of evidence--in this case,
historical data.

You will notice that Helmreich has chosen to provide evidence only
for positive stereotypes. In the second paragraph he names several negative stereotypes but declines to elaborate on them. I think we are well
advised to follow his example in making writing assignments. Although
I've included "dumb jocks," "Jewish mothers," and "greedy businessmen" on
my list, I have discovered that in fulfilling these assignments students
treat such stereotypes humorously, or they give solid reasons for the per-
sistence of the stereotype, reasons that serve to exonerate the subject.
This is not to say, of course, that negative stereotypes contain no truth,
but both students and instructor are probably better off for abstaining
from attacks that reinforce negative attitudes toward classmates.

Ruth Hubbard, "Test-Tube Babies: Solution or Problem?" (p. 365)

Hubbard's essay is a forthright policy claim, a two-pronged attack
on the process of in vitro fertilization. As a biologist, she warns us
of the health dangers to both mother and fetus. As a feminist and a liberal, she is opposed to the view that women, in order to be fulfilled,
must bear their own children and equally opposed to the investment of
large sums of money that might be better spent in satisfying pressing social needs.

The essay is clearly organized. The first part introduces the subject by describing the process--for student writers the lesson here is
that any claim about a process must begin with an understandable description of that process. At the end of this description Hubbard states her
opposition, with the rest of the essay giving the reasons for her opposition. In the second part she outlines the health risks. In the third
part she attacks the view that women in our society are expected to bear

children. In the fourth part she argues that the money spent on developing this process should be devoted instead to providing jobs, food, housing, and medical care for those who need it.

Although in vitro fertilization is a complicated subject involving a number of complicated issues, Hubbard's presentation is admirably lucid, in its expression as well as its organization. Students should have no difficulty understanding her argument. They should also have no difficulty discovering her values--as a feminist and a liberal.

They may, however, want to take issue with some of her assumptions. Many medical procedures are risky in their infancy. Should they therefore be abandoned? Is it still true that women in our society must have babies in order to be fulfilled? (This essay was written in 1977.) Do most infertile women have the option of adopting? Hubbard urges that we should try to change the practices that make adoption difficult. But such changes, if they come, will not come within the lifetimes of most women who want children now. If the money being spent on in vitro technology is withdrawn, will it necessarily be allocated to the social needs to which Hubbard gives priority?

Hubbard uses vivid examples--the tragedies associated with the use of DES and thalidomide, the ways in which women have been socialized to bear children--to support her claims. Students should be required to provide examples, as Hubbard does, to confirm their own claims.

Martin Luther King, Jr., "I Have a Dream" (p. 371)

Someone in the class, whether instructor or student, who can muster a compelling declamatory style, should read part of this speech aloud. If you can obtain a recording of the original speech, so much the better. There is no better way to savor the language and to gain some understanding, however limited, of the impact of this speech on its listeners. Ask students to compare, as far as possible, its effect when read and its effect when listened to. Is there a difference? If so, how great is it? How do you account for the difference? (There is no doubt that the human voice, with its timbre and its capacity for emotional expression, can indicate values as effectively as words.) Students should also keep in mind that this speech was delivered before a large outdoor crowd. Would this situation influence the kind of argument King needed to make?

Students should be asked to consider this speech as a written argument. What was the purpose of this speech? How specific was King in recommending policy or actions to be undertaken by the audience? Would the speech have been more effective as argument if King had urged the enactment of specific laws and exhorted his audience to work for them?

Finally, students should attend to the language. Does the language enhance the impact of the argument? Or does it sometimes distract? For example, in the fourth paragraph, there is the sustained metaphor of the promissory note. But the succeeding sentences contain figures of speech involving drugs, valleys, sunlit paths, open doors, quicksand, and rocks. Are some metaphors more effective than others? If so, why?

Most students, alas, will no longer recognize the biblical comparisons in the repetitions and parallel structures. The instructor may point them out and ask about the inferences to be drawn from them.

John Leo, "Homosexuality: Tolerance Versus Approval" (p. 376)

The subject of the treatment of homosexuals can rouse intense feelings. Leo's article may therefore be the most controversial in the book.

The first part of the essay offers Leo an opportunity to demonstrate his own fairness; he effectively demolishes three of the popular reasons for disapproval of homosexuals. There is good use of evidence--history, statistics, expert opinion--although some of his information about the origins of homosexuality may now be out of date. Students may need to learn who Kinsey is and why Leo expects his readers to be able to identify him. They may also need to be given some minimal information about Freud and why he is mentioned in this context.

The most provocative issue raised by Leo is a value warrant: that the function of government is "not to guarantee jobs or apartments for every disaffected group in society but only to step in where systematic or massive discrimination requires it." In the next-to-last paragraph, Leo repeats his principle: "The Government has better things to do than proliferate categories of unfireable citizens. Like Masons, millenarians, and est graduates, homosexuals must take their chances in the marketplace, just as everyone else does." (The issue will, of course, be easier to argue if students can identify the three groups mentioned.) Although the subject of the function of government is broad and complex and students may not have thought about it sufficiently to make profound judgments, a discussion of homosexual rights may be a useful introduction to a number of pertinent issues surrounding the subject.

Students can refer to the arguments on affirmative action in "Opposing Viewpoints." According to Leo, homosexuals are, in effect, asking for affirmative action, that is, protective laws guaranteeing certain rights in employment. Leo distinguishes between blacks and women, on the one hand--groups who have been severely discriminated against in the past--and homosexuals, on the other, who are "already well integrated into the economy." A discussion question in the book asks whether this is a reasonable distinction.

If there is an organization of homosexuals on campus, a representative may be invited to appear before the class to argue against Leo's assumptions about the relationship between homosexuals and government protection, or to challenge some of Leo's data.

(text pages 383-386)

Michael Levin, "The Case for Torture" (p. 383)

Levin's value claim--that it is not only right but mandatory to torture terrorists in extreme cases--will come as a shock to most readers. But I suspect (unfairly?) that for some the shock will be perfunctory, a concession to the humanity we are all <u>supposed</u> to feel as moral human beings. Levin deals in a treatment of subjects likely to outrage many readers. He is the author of "How to Tell Bad from Worse" in the chapter on definition, an article also calculated to arouse disagreement. One of his most controversial claims appears in an article called "Is Racial Discrimination Special?" (He is not, however, the author of "The Springsteening of Disarmament," written by another Michael Levin.)

As a philosopher Levin knows how to move the reader step by step through the argument in a modified Socratic questioning, which may compel the reader who opposes Levin to give away his own argument as he follows his.

The examples are exceptionally vivid and appropriate. As writers of arguments, students can absorb at least one salutary lesson from this essay. Whether they accept Levin's claim, they may take note of the way in which his examples--an atomic bomb on Manhattan Island, a bomb planted on a plane, the kidnapping of an infant, the possible assassination of Hitler--force the reader to face the implications of his choices. Throughout the writing course we try to convince students of the necessity for developing, not merely stating, their theses. Levin shows them one striking way of doing this. Without these examples, Levin's assumptions would surely be less convincing--they would also, I think, lose their moral conviction.

Levin's argument connects at certain points with the arguments in favor of capital punishment. That is, despite the moral revulsion we may feel in participating in the execution of another human being, we may conclude that this barbarous act is justified in the cause of a higher good. Ernest Van den Haag, a proponent of capital punishment, says that some pacifists, when asked if they would continue to oppose capital punishment even if it were decisively proved to be a deterrent to crime, have answered that they would continue to oppose it nevertheless. Here is a nice distinction, then, between two ways of thinking about extreme penalties and their consequences.

Walter Lippmann, "The Indispensable Opposition" (p. 387)

Lippmann offers a number of striking examples to clarify his generalizations, but students will still need to read this essay with special
care, first because Lippmann's sentences are long and carry a heavy burden
of meaning, and second because the thesis will be unfamiliar.

First, as writing teachers we are not in the specific business of
teaching students to read; rather we assume that college students come to
our classes equipped to read any material written for a literate person.
Nevertheless, in order to discuss Lippmann intelligently, we will have to
examine single sentences that may give trouble, e.g., the second long sentence in the fifth paragraph. We will need to paraphrase and interpret,
to encourage students to ask questions about passages that remain obscure.
There are also places where historical references will have to be ex-
plained: the new Emperor of Ethiopia, Voltaire, Magna Carta.

Second, students may, in fact, interpret Lippmann to mean just the
opposite of what he argues; they may continue to assert Lippmann thinks
free speech means toleration of the opposition. I think that the careless
or inaccurate interpretation of texts is often due to the inability of the
reader to substitute a new belief for one that he has subscribed to for a
long time. As soon, therefore, as students see the words "free speech,"
the old meanings concerning the right to speak leap up to block the passage of new ones.

It should be possible to lead students to consider the validity of
Lippmann's claim by 1) warning them that the thesis of this essay may be
new to them; 2) asking them to attend to his examples, especially the
splendid one of the doctor, which is repeated in several places; and 3)
suggesting they consult their own experience. On many college campuses
the principle of free speech, in Lippmann's meaning, is violated when
speakers with unpopular views are shouted down or flagrantly ignored.
Students may be able to recall and analyze such events. Moreover, they
should be able to find instances in their own lives when being forced to
listen to disagreeable opposing views brought them closer to some important truth.

H. L. Mencken, "The Penalty of Death" (p. 394)

As an argument in favor of capital punishment--if that is what it
is--Mencken's little essay is by no means the most convincing that

students may read. In fact, it offers students an opportunity to uncover lapses in the thinking of one of the most formidable critics of American life.

First of all, the organization of the essay is somewhat distorted. Half is devoted to a definition of catharsis and its function in the punishment inflicted for noncapital crimes. The discussion of capital punishment comes almost as an afterthought. Even the transitional sentence, "I know of no public demand for the death penalty for ordinary crimes, even for ordinary homicides," suggests that Mencken's real interest in this essay lies in the discussion of catharsis as an incentive for all kinds of punishment, not necessarily the penalty of death.

Then there is the question of Mencken's attitude toward "katharsis." In one statement he alleges his neutrality: "I do not argue that this yearning is noble; I simply argue that it is almost universal among human beings." At the same time, however, he refers to it as a "healthy" letting off of steam. And the use of catharsis as Aristotle used it, rather than of the term "revenge," which he rejects, suggests that Mencken regards this emotion as desirable. On the other hand, Mencken disapproves of the prolonged suffering of the criminal--although the thought of his suffering was precisely what the victims were meant to enjoy in their pursuit of catharsis.

Mencken's description of the psychological response as a "healthy letting off of steam" brings us to still another problem that students may be less capable of judging--the tone of the essay. Mencken was a justly celebrated wit, but his tone is often one of sneering contempt for the foibles of timorous and ignorant mankind. In this essay we recognize a tone that might be characterized as mildly offensive--facetious about an event that most readers, including those in favor of capital punishment, would hardly describe as "wafting the criminal to realms of bliss." Even the use of "katharsis," the purging of emotions through a play, may seem an inappropriate way to characterize the emotions of people confronting the death of a real person.

Students may wish to compare the tone in Mencken with that of such advocates of capital punishment as Walter Berns, Ernest van den Haag, and James Q. Wilson, who argue that the necessity for capital punishment is based on justice and the right of a moral society to exact the ultimate penalty in extreme cases.

As for his claim in the last part of the essay, Mencken must have known that the postponement of death almost always occurs at the request of the prisoner or his advocates, not as a means of allowing the criminal to make his peace with God. And here, too, Mencken cannot resist a somewhat tasteless gibe at God's capacity to forgive.

(text pages 398-416)

George Orwell, "Politics and the English Language" (p. 398)

I find that Orwell's great essay grows more and more difficult to
teach as our students become less and less sensitive to language and
style. In the chapter on language, I have included some examples of in-
flated language that confirm Orwell's criticism. The deficiencies of
these professional writers are not, however, those of which freshmen students are guilty in their own writing. Rather, the examples represent the
kinds of obscure and pretentious language that students should be alert to
in the arguments that they read.

In order to read Orwell intelligently, students must not only understand his terms--"dying metaphors," "verbal false limbs," "pretentious
diction"--but also be able to appreciate the awkwardness and unintelligi-
bility in his examples. If I discover that students are not responsive to
these problems, I move on.

The organization of the essay, fortunately, lends itself to a study
of discrete parts without a loss of sense or purpose. As teachers of argument, we should give our greatest attention to those parts that have a
direct relevance to the way in which bad language can distort an argument.
Under "Meaningless Words," for example, Orwell uses selections from politics. But the heart of the essay may fairly be said to begin with the
second paragraph (13) on page 405. I would, therefore, concentrate on an
understanding of Orwell's claim about the relationship between politics
and language. For this more examples are crucial (Orwell offers only
phrases). There are brief selections in the chapter on language to which
students may refer. The best long examples will usually be found in the
writing and speeches of partisans on the far right and the far left of the
political spectrum. You may have to begin by bringing in examples you
have found that show what is meant by distortion and deception in political language. Freshman students may not know enough about the history
and circumstances surrounding a particular argument to detect its misuse
of language. Perhaps some egregious outburst in the school paper will
serve.

Noel Perrin, "The War of the Woods" (p. 411)

Perrin's essay is a splendid example of the form of organization described in the Appendix as "Refuting the Opposing View." After disposing
of three possible explanations for the differences between snowmobiling

47

or skiing, he offers his own theory in the eighth paragraph: "One is a great deal more work than the other." Part of the essay will be devoted to providing reasons why country people and urbanites choose their respective sports according to how much work they require. In Perrin's terms, the Principle of the Conservation of Energy is opposed to the Principle of Hard Play.

But these opposing theories are not all he wishes to explore. At the end he introduces a criticism of the urbanites or middle-class skiers with their "assumptions of moral superiority." In this final discussion he comes down on the side of the snowmobilers and the country people who have found a wonderful release from the hardships of their working lives. Perrin's essay is a value claim that establishes the criticism of snowmobilers by skiers as unjustified. As in most good value claims, the first part of the argument provides a factual basis for the claim.

There are several exemplary lessons for student writers in this essay. One is Perrin's use of personal experience, not to the exclusion of other kinds of evidence, but sufficient for giving authority to his claims. His anecdotes are both amusing and insightful. Equally persuasive is his double life as a middle-class teacher and a countryman who can understand and explain both arguments. But there is also an abundance of brilliant, easily assimilable details and images, even for those readers who have never skied or never rode a snowmobile, who have lived in sunny climates where such recreations are unknown.

Perrin's language is a happy combination of the colloquial with its contractions and familiar expressions--"But that won't wash"--and the graceful, using long complex sentences and parallel constructions.

Plato, "Socrates to His Accusers" (p. 417)

Both the language in this translation and the beliefs expressed by Socrates will strike some students as archaic. Perhaps the problem weighing most heavily on them in their first reading will be the length of the paragraphs. Here we may help students to cope with the density by asking them to read for paragraphing, that is, to break up the long passages by inserting their own beginnings and endings.

The most provocative issue raised by Socrates is his objection to the coward's insistence on escaping death through dishonorable compromise or surrender: "For neither in war nor yet at law ought any man to use every way of escaping death." Somewhat to my surprise I have discovered that this sentiment does not strike all students as admirable or even sensible. In their attempts to define heroism some students will reveal that they subscribe to the old adage, "Better a live coward than a dead hero." They will deny that Socrates is a hero for choosing death rather than saying what his accusers wanted him to say. (Does the fact that

Socrates believes firmly in a sweet afterlife diminish the heroism of his
suicide?)

Heroism will, in fact, prove to be one of the most difficult concepts
for students to define. As in all definitions of vague or ambiguous
terms, examples serve to clarify for students the principles on which
their definitions rest. (See Levin's "The Case for Torture" for such examples.) If students are familiar with the case of Galileo, who, unlike
Socrates, elected to recant rather than suffer severe punishment, perhaps
death, they might try to contrast the two actions and offer value judgments about them based on their definitions. Students should also be
asked to reflect on the consequences for society of the decision they
would advise either Socrates or Galileo to make.

Even the apparently archaic beliefs about oracles and death are related to contemporary issues in which most students take an ongoing interest. The oracle that persuaded Socrates that what had happened to him was
good is not different in kind from our own hunches ("the familiar oracle
within me") or the astrological charts that millions of people consult
every day. Can students make anything of Socrates's "good cheer about
death"? (Hazlitt alleged that young men do not believe that they will
ever die.) Do they take seriously Socrates's belief in a world beyond the
present one, where he either sleeps pleasantly or is permitted to continue
his pursuit of knowledge and to sojourn with the great heroes, writers,
and judges of the past? Some students will confess to a belief in an
afterlife, but it probably will not take the form Socrates envisions.
Like the game of Who-Shall-Survive-the-Nuclear-Holocaust? a description of
the afterlife can reveal a good deal about our assumptions and our values.

Jonathan Swift, "A Modest Proposal" (p. 421)

If students are reading this essay for the first time without prepar-
ation or warning, some of them will take Swift's proposal literally. But,
then, so did some seventeenth-century readers with perhaps less justification. Some teachers think that the multiple horrors of organized cruel-
ty and genocide in the twentieth century have made Swift's proposal at
least marginally credible. We hope not.

Students should be able to describe the person ostensibly making
the modest proposal, since the proposer himself calls attention to his
characteristics: compassionate but disinterested, thoughtful, reasonable,
temperate, well-informed. The question is whether such a person--one who
is compassionate and reasonable--could make a proposal to breed human infants for food. If students agree that he could not, then why has he
done so? If his reasons are not those that he alleges them to be, what
can they be?

There are several ways of deciding on the answers. One is to examine the language. Does the voice of the proposer--formal, detached,

heavy with statistical data--suggest one who is passionately distressed by
the suffering of the Irish? Why does the proposer refer to the Irish in
terms descriptive of animals rather than human beings? Is there any place
in which the voice and language of the author seem to change, where he offers solutions entirely different in kind from the breeding of children
for food? How are we to interpret the difference in these two voices? In
the next-to-last paragraph even the voice of the proposer begins to change;
to urge that Irish adults would have been fortunate to die within the
first year of life is a judgment that can be offered only in bitter irony.
    It is not just the language or the disparity between the voices which
can give away the ironic stance. There are also the external criteria,
including the subject itself. Are there people in Swift's audience, no
matter how indifferent to the fate of the Irish, who would enjoy the pros-
pect of eating human infants? Would an Anglican dean be likely to make
such a suggestion in the expectation that reasonable people would find it
acceptable? Why would an essay outlining a serious proposal to breed
children for food survive for more than two hundred years not as a curios-
ity but as a model of expository prose for readers throughout the English-
speaking world? Consideration of these questions ought to lead to a sus-
picion, even in the most undiscerning reader, that some other interpretation than the literal one must exist.

Lewis Thomas, "The Health-Care System" (p. 430)

    Thomas's argument may be interpreted as largely factual in proving
that we are far healthier than we think and that our hypochondria puts an
increasingly severe strain on our health-care resources. As in other
factual claims, both values and policy also emerge. Thomas condemns the
media and the food and publishing industries for their vociferous and mis-
leading promotion of health products, and his final paragraph suggests
that we should worry about more pressing problems than nonexistent dangers
to personal health. It is also possible to emphasize the proposal at the
end and treat this essay primarily as a claim of policy supported by solid
data about the real state of our health.
    Wherever Thomas offers evidence it is clear and specific, but not
every generalization is developed. In places Thomas seems to expect that
his readers share his beliefs and supply their own evidence: "Pollutants
. . . are being worried about lest they cause cancer in us, for heaven's
sake."
    Although the argument may be based on an authority warrant--Thomas
is, after all, a preeminent authority in the field of health and health-
care--there will be students who think that Thomas's optimism is un-
founded. They may want to argue that he is not sufficiently concerned
about pollution, or that the health-food industry serves a useful pur-
pose--both good subjects for factual claims.

Finally, students should recognize that Thomas's great popularity is due in large part to a clear, readable style that recalls the conversation of a wise and learned friend.

Gore Vidal, "Drugs" (p. 434)

Vidal's claim that people should be free to use drugs is no longer new nor was it first, but his restatement is welcome, given his refreshing testiness and frank assumption of moral superiority. His tone may be compared to Mencken's, and like the earlier writer, Vidal is also an eloquent and acerbic critic of human foibles. Here he laments the inability of Americans to remember "anything that happened before last Tuesday," but his sarcasm seems more appropriate to an argument about drugs than to one about capital punishment.

The warrant underlying Vidal's claim should not be difficult for students to extract: "Each man has the right to do what he wants with his own life as long as he does not interfere with his neighbor's pursuit of happiness." Compare this to Leo's assumptions about government, which, although framed in different terms, also regard government interference in private concerns (here the hiring of workers) as unjustified. Or refer to the arguments on euthanasia in "Opposing Viewpoints." Vidal says, "Every man . . . has the power (and should have the legal right) to kill himself if he chooses." In the section on euthanasia, students will find arguments favoring the right of people to end their lives. They will also encounter the argument that such a right belongs only to the state. These ethical questions go beyond the use of drugs and offer a broad field for discussion and writing.

If they understand the references ("Fu Manchu theory," "silent majority," "friendly playground pushers") students should enjoy Vidal's humor. Ask them how they respond to a humorous treatment of a serious subject. Does it undercut or reinforce the claim? (The Purdue Reports tell us that high school students will express opposition to most of the rights in the Bill of Rights without knowing their origins.)

Bibliography on the Toulmin Model

Listed below are articles by teachers of composition, rhetoric, speech, and debate that explain and apply the Toulmin model for use in the classroom.

Brockriede, Wayne, and Douglas Ehninger. "Toulmin on Argument: An Interpretation and Application." The Quarterly Journal of Speech, 46 (1960), 44-53. The authors interpret the Toulmin model as presented in Toulmin's The Uses of Argument. They clearly define each element of the model and explain its advantages over traditional systems of logic.

Christenson, Thomas, and Paul R. Nelson. "The Toulmin Model: Asset and Millstone." In David A. Thomas (Ed.), Advanced Debate: Readings in Theory, Practice and Teaching. Skokie, IL: National Textbook, 1975, 228-234. The authors provide a clear summary of Toulmin, distinguishing between the "basic" model--claim, data, and warrant--and the "expanded" model, which introduces the other elements of backing, reservation, and qualifier.

Kaufer, David S., and Christine M. Neuwirth. "Integrating Formal Logic and the New Rhetoric: A Four-Stage Heuristic." College English, 45 (1983), 380-389. The authors argue that formal logic can be used to supplement insights from the new rhetoric (as put forth by Toulmin and others), believing that an argument should be tested for its deductive certainty as well as for the plausibility of its premises. They provide a four-stage model for teaching students how to integrate logical and probabilistic reasoning in arguments.

Kneupper, Charles W. "Teaching Argument: An Introduction to the Toulmin Model." College Composition and Communication, 29 (1978), 237-241.

Kneupper begins with an attack on the use of logic and fallacies as a means of teaching argumentative composition. He offers a brief summary of Toulmin's model as a superior method, then applies the model to the first paragraph of Thoreau's Civil Disobedience, diagramming the argument in simplified form. He emphasizes that for students "how they are arguing will be clearer," and they will be able to see relationships between parts of the argument.

Stratman, James F. "Teaching Written Argument: The Significance of Toulmin's Layout for Sentence-Combining." College English, 48 (1982), 718-733. The author believes that in using Toulmin's "layout" for argument in sentence-combining, students can learn new syntactic patterns. They can learn "skills appropriate to argument--estimating the relevance of facts, assessing validity, and planning refutations based on premises shared with an opponent." For example, one way of helping students to learn the function and importance of warrants is to have them adapt such warrants explicitly in a sentence-combining exercise. "Toulmin's layout can reveal how syntactic transformations strengthen or weaken the structure implicit in argumentative exercises by revealing changes in the underlying relations between 'claim' and 'evidence' that these transformations may entail." A complicated analysis but thought-provoking.

Trent, Jimmie D. "Toulmin's Model of an Argument: An Examination and Extension." The Quarterly Journal of Speech, 54 (1968), 252-259. Trent views Toulmin's model as a supplement to syllogistic reasoning. He nevertheless argues that Toulmin presents arguments more clearly and accurately than the classical syllogism.

Several textbooks on writing, speech, and debate explain and apply the Toulmin model. A few are listed below.

Ehninger, Douglas. Influence, Belief, and Argument: An Introduction to Responsible Persuasion. Glenview, IL: Scott, Foresman, 1974. This book explains the Toulmin model and includes suggestions after each chapter for additional reading.

Ehninger, Douglas, and Wayne Brockriede. Decision by Debate. 2d ed. New York: Harper & Row, 1978. This book includes a comprehensive summary of the Toulmin model along with suggestions after each chapter for further reading.

MCroskey, James C. An Introduction to Rhetorical Communication. 4th ed. Englewood Cliffs, NJ: Prentice-Hall, Inc., 1982.

Makay, John J. Speaking with an Audience: Communicating Ideas and Attitudes. New York: Harper & Row, 1977.

Bibliography

Rieke, Richard D., and Malcolm O. Sillars. Argumentation and the Decision-Making Process. New York: Wiley, 1975.

Sproule, J. Michael. Argument: Language and its Influence. New York: McGraw-Hill, 1980. This book includes a list of references on argument.

Toulmin, Steven, Richard Rieke, and Allan Janik. An Introduction to Reasoning. 2d ed. New York: Macmillan, 1984.

Zacharis, John C., and Coleman C. Bender. Speech Communications: A Rational Approach. New York: Wiley, 1976. This book includes additional readings after each chapter.

Bedford Books *of* St. Martin's Press